Of Moments and Days

Graham Wood

Of Moments and Days

For Murray and Nick

Of Moments and Days
ISBN 978 1 76109 528 3
Copyright © text Graham Wood 2023
Cover image: painting by David Hope
Peg whorl photo, page 38: Tim Milkins

First published 2023 by
GINNINDERRA PRESS
PO Box 3461 Port Adelaide 5015
www.ginninderrapress.com.au

Contents

Wings Across the Sunset	9
Moments in Chorus	10
Bush Angels, Christmas	12
Eating Mandarins	13
Afternoon at Bobbin Head	14
House of the Terracotta Warrior	15
Flying	16
The Bottom Line	17
The Sun in June	18
Seven Years Widowed	19
First Gig at Wanchai	20
Centenary	21
Our Sixth Palindromic	22
In the Slumbering Dark	23
The Gorgonzola Salad	24
The Currency of Teeth	25
Unfolding	26
A Traveller Asks a Prophet for Advice by the Turning of the Road	27
Midnight and Thirty-two Maharajahs	28
Man in the Mall with Flowers	29
The Marry-Go-Round	30
Painting the Edges	31
Orientallan	32
My Son from the South	33
Cadet Day English Lesson	34
Poem Pruning	35
Film Fruit	36
Chas. Conder's Holiday	37
Peg Whorl	39
These Artful Tarts	40

Is There Any News?	41
Policy Launch	42
The Visit from the Queen	43
The Day that Gough Got In	44
With a Small Pencil	45
Small Things	46
Nothing Lasts	48
Picking Up the Sun	49
Ontological Ouch!	50
How to Make a Romantic Poet	51
Aegean Blue	53
Eternity – passing the baton	54
Islands of the Circle	55
Avocado Eve	56
The Emperor of Fish	57
Cat Ritual	58
Felinity	59
The Undeep Desk	60
The Woman Who Had Her Head Detached	61
Crows in the City	62
The Courtesan and the Poet	63
Freedom's Gate	64
That Summer of the Bicentenary	66
Bitter Days	67
Perhaps You Went Quietly	68
Last Vacation	69
Love in the Time of Coronavirus	70
You on Patmos	71
Town of Boeotia	73
Postcard From Tuscany	74
Barbarians Inside the Gates	75
Standing Stones	76

Killin	78
Poolside at the Bali Grand	79
The Next Island	81
Beijing Ascending	82
Tai Hu	83
The Open Window	84
Other Voices	85
On the Chemo	93
Borrowed Time	94
The Idea of God	95
The Universe Within	96
Still Clasped About the Stone	97
Termite	98
Dark Harbour	101
Last Light	102
The Art of Hoping	103
Acknowledgements	107

'O aching time! O moments big as years!'
– John Keats (*Hyperion*, Book 1, line 64)

'We do not remember days, we remember moments.
The richness of life lies in memories we have forgotten.'
– Cesare Pavese, *The Business of Living – Diaries 1935–1950*

Wings Across the Sunset

Pincio Gardens, Rome

These wings across the sunset cast
their gracenotes on the sky,
passing in perfect silence.
Another night comes on and time
plays tricks with us. We insist
on measuring its passage like music
pretending regularity in its ceaseless flow,
an imagined rhythm beating in equal
increments from either side of now
out towards two infinities.

Zeno might agree with that, but not Einstein
and not my heart. Time can speed up
and slow down; on occasion it can stand
like a frozen body of water so completely still
that one moment sweeps all others up inside it.
Then we are absorbed by time itself, able to walk
out upon its surface and watch ourselves
struggle into being or begin to disappear.

Moments in Chorus

1.

The mind is a cafeteria
full of ravenous memories
always rattling cutlery.
Are they ever satisfied?

2.

What moment is this slinking in,
warming briefly, but too hot
to hold and keep?
What right have memories to intrude
and haunt us in our solitude?

3.

Strange, this love of the vanished moment,
the song of the idle life, buoyed on a breath
so thinly compromised,
so enchantingly distressed
that memory struggles to recapture
forgotten things, raking the moment over,
remaking it.

4.

What hope can these days rekindle
amongst the debris of the intervening years,
and what use? To revive in solitude the strain
of an instant long-trammelled by mundanities:
work and sleep, the sour meal of years.

5.

Release joy unbidden
whenever you please –
enough of the downside,
warm wind through the trees!

Bush Angels, Christmas

From passing train
        garlanded
two angels stand:
        roughcast
homespun –
        tyres and hessian
clothing spines
        of sapling.

Between bush angels
        three children
cartwheel,
        cavort with branch
and mistletoe
        through loose shade
of summer gums.

There appeared
        almost
five children at play
        as the window
passed
        and slid away –
and all
        of them
                it seemed
had wings.

Eating Mandarins

Mandarins bring my grandmother back every time,
standing together by the old house in winter sunlight
sharing the first fruit I remember. Four years old,
I'd wrestled it moments before from the huge tree
in the chookyard as she held me up towards it,
one of many plump tangerine disks
bobbing overhead against a sea of green.

She rolled the peel off deftly with her fingers, turning it on the point
of one thumb into large orange scoops of rind, stripping each pod
free of its pulpy strings. Then it was there! A burst of sweetness
on my tongue, elemental, never before anything like this.

Half a century dead my grandmother now,
inhabiting the long sweet breath of memory.
In spite of the decades that have vanished,
every time I peel and savour this favoured fruit
my grandmother is with me talking softly,
sharing the same mandarin.

Afternoon at Bobbin Head

For Nick

As they walk to the bay, they talk
of fish, bait, tackle: boy things
of the hunt and other paraphernalia.
Then out they wade, waist deep
in salt summer water, laughing,
trailing drift paths of spume. All around
in the sheltered inlet fish jump –
mullet glint and plop, the surface shakes
and ripples out again to flatness.

The two boys wade and cast,
their voices carrying over shallow water
shot with reflected sand. Behind them,
a cliff of eucalypts soars sharply upward
crowning them against the western bank
with a rising wall of gums, angophoras,
sandstone honeycombed among trees –
a vertical updraft from a level surface
the patina of liquid gold.

Over the deep afternoon
the colour fades, melts and thins,
leaches away beneath encroaching shadows.
When, from the low tide of mangroves
I beckon them back over darkened water,
the high cliff has blanketed all sun from the bay.
The surface is only shadows now, but underneath
hidden gold, remembered laughter, a treasured day.

House of the Terracotta Warrior

To the grand-girls all

To the house of the terracotta warrior
the grand-girls come, saying hello
to him in their little voices, goodbye
as they leave. He watches them
come and go, the seasons change,
the girls grow bigger. And sometimes,
beneath his veil of bird droppings, I bear
witness to the faintest shift of smile
on his impassive ochre face.

Flying

The creek in my street is in flood.
I pause and remember your father,
the words he said about its course
the only time we met.
He spoke of the flow of water,
the slope of hillside down my street,
the local rise and fall of land
as though some interior geography
transposed terrain beneath him.
Even out walking, he saw the land look up,
dreamed of landscapes he once knew well –
Poona or Ponca City moving under his wings
and rising up to meet him
as he touched the earth again.

Now the months begin to run in years
but pausing at the creek in flood,
I shake his throttle hand once more
and hear his voice describe my suburb
with a pilot's eye. Exultant,
his memory soars above us still.

The Bottom Line

My aunt remembers her father, my grandfather,
carrying only two suitcases when he set out
for his last home. With tears in her eyes
sitting amongst her boxes and chests,
she fears already that she too
is bound on that journey.
She remarks that now
she has little need
of things, possessions.

Life like a bell curve pulls us
up and away from the bottom line,
cementing us about with things
until it draws us down again
almost unburdened,
as we began.

The Sun in June

For my mother

The June sun flooding through my windows
lit up your fine hair
like a circle of light.

I photographed you that morning
on my sofa, your face half-vanishing
in winter sun.

Your smile was brighter than the light
behind you, but not enough to banish
the worry from your eyes.

My heart's too full tonight to settle,
remembering you that morning, the last day
we had you whole and well.

Seven Years Widowed

Seven years widowed, my mother
sits twisting her wedding ring in the sun,
happier almost than she's ever been.
Warm and drowsy this morning,
she sits on the veranda drying her hair,
drinking tea over the crosswords,
toying from habit with her wedding band.

Whenever had she been as free as this?
In her early twenties certainly,
between parents and husband,
before marriage and children,
with a circle of friends as wide as now
and some of them the same.
There are sons who speak on the phone
most days or most weeks, and visit
when their lives allow. Once more
she has books and music, songs
to sing freely at the edge of chores,
a life with choices possible again.

Now on the veranda of the house
built as he wanted for his retirement,
she has been free for seven years
and happy almost, except for the ring.

First Gig at Wanchai

For Murray

I went to watch you growl your urban roar
at Wanchai, front the band defiant,
pump the crowd to frenzy in a small bar
filled with smoke. This rough music
translates with you to Asia, belts out
through smoky grunge and smell of beer
to passers-by on Jaffe Road and bargirls
plying trade. I move to your rhythm,
beat to your pulse, the thump and whistle
of the crowd, the shake of basement notes
deep underground…and watch you
pounding centre-stage in front of me,
your booted feet in thud,
in full growl punching air.

Centenary

IM Athol Powys Fowler, youngest great-uncle

If your life had not been taken early by the great powers of Europe
blundering into the 20th century, we might have known each other
when I was a child. I remember your eldest brother
when he was an old man, 23 years your senior, who survived
the Western Front with only the top of one thumb blown off.
You were not so lucky – the shrapnel that hit you
took your arm and shoulder clean off in the mud of Lagnicourt
and you succumbed to the inevitable two days beyond that.
They buried you behind the village where you died,
the church bells marking time for you since then.

What remains of you today, half the world away in another century?
Only one or two small effects, three photographs, a Dead Man's Penny
and some family stories. Alas, I feared you were ceasing to live
even in memory until the Armistice centenary that November,
when a busload of Aussies pulled up to say G'day, and left a flag
and gum leaves at your grave. They took your story away with them
your name and gravestone in their cameras, and found you
on the official website with one Canadian, the only burials
not from the United Kingdom in that small war cemetery.
They read your name, touched your headstone, shed tears for you
and photographed themselves behind your grave, kneeling.
A century on, repatriation of sorts as these pilgrims
in homage bear your memory home.

Our Sixth Palindromic

For Wayne and Warwick

Last year and this, eleven years
in the making, we celebrate
between us our sixth palindromic,
knowing not too many lie ahead.
Well along our road now, our own
Route 66, we travel like Kerouac and Joad
heading west, taking advantage of the vistas,
the abundancy of rest stops, and the gradual
fine-tuning of habitual rhythms
to the spirit of our times. We remain
unsettled, though chuffed of course,
by the curious glances of younger roadies
marvelling at our state of preservation.

In the Slumbering Dark

Free of dreaming or remembering it,
there have been no nightmares since childhood
when, very young, he screamed awake
one Christmas Eve to find Santa Claus
leaping out maniacally from behind the tree,
sluicing him with red paint,
bucket after bucket. Despite that,
he's never woken once in adult fear
or confusion, nor suffered the pangs
of acute embarrassment as the star attraction
in countless irrational scenarios.

Undercover each night, sleeping calmly
through the deepest hours of the dark,
he has no knowledge of the black pool
where the banshees howl, nor
the ragged gullies that throb and gush
with sudden blood, nor even the shock
of total nakedness in the midst
of astonished peers.

Each night untroubled, every night except one,
he sleeps through the dark forests of fairy tale
waking to each succeeding sunrise
rested and unperturbed.
On Christmas Eve, he never sleeps at all.

The Gorgonzola Salad

We argued over the salad as we always argue,
each of us contesting a host of trivial things:
who should begin and when?
Would fork or finger do?
Who should or shouldn't pluck
choice morsels from the tangle of rucola?

Unlike many of our barneys, this one
persists in memory, endures
like a clip from silent cinema
unreeling itself on a never-ending loop.
I continue doggedly to eat against your wishes
swallowing invective with every bite,
stoning you with belligerent silence.
Across the table meanwhile, beyond
the confection of green foliage, brown walnuts
and toasted gorgonzola, you launch into me,
eyebrows twitching and hair back-lit, alive –
your halo of spitting snakes vipering me still.

The Currency of Teeth

Teeth stay put unless
they are pushed out by others,
or come to grief in myriad ways.
Some last decades, until
from dearth of daily brushing,
they clog and choke, and are themselves
eaten from without or from within.
Some indeed stay put almost till the end
when they fall from their gummy perch
after a lifetime of chomp and grind.
Other hardy ones outlast their owners
to perish in flames, or encased in earth,
lie in weight for thieves or archaeologists.

But early on, from the bottom of watery tumblers,
fallen baby teeth leer drunkenly at passing parents,
expecting a troupe of cashed–up fairies
jingling change at night. Teeth
are juvenile currency after all, highly negotiable
on the first deal like prime financial instruments,
but after that, the supply is limited
and the going rate inflates
with every fallen molar.

Unfolding

At the blurred edges of the day
you unfold, sweep me
with the softness locked inside,
shelled against the workday.
At dawn the folds have yet
to line your face, and at dusk
the hard creases relax, fade
feint
as
margins
on
a
blank
page
softly lined with blue.

A Traveller Asks a Prophet for Advice by the Turning of the Road

Can you tell me,
he asked the prophet
by the turning of the road,
whether this woman
is the one
worth every risk?

He asked once more
into the peace
surrounding the prophet,
into the pervading stillness:
Is this the time?
Is here the place?
Is she the one?

And slowly
after long silence
the prophet answered.
It was as though
his heart began to speak:
'Surrender,' the prophet said. 'Listen.'
Then in the whisperings of his soul
three words came, insistent and clear:
Now,
Here,
Her.

Midnight and Thirty-two Maharajahs

For Rosemary – Jodhpur, Rajasthan

Midnight, and thirty-two maharajahs
look down from the family pedigree,
corralled above you while you sleep.
On the mantel, a clock ticks in quiet
syncopation with your breathing;
tomorrow and our departure edge
their way towards the dawn.
Here, this night
you've notched up fifty years
serene in sleep below these royal ghosts,
oblivious of their chequered past.
Thirty-two maharajahs above your head –
and your father met the second last!
Tonight beside you in this king-size bed
I gauge my wealth above these kings –
I'd give my weight in gold for you.

Note: on high ceremonial occasions, some Indian maharajahs were known to weigh themselves in public and distribute an equivalent weight of gold and jewels among their subjects.

Man in the Mall with Flowers

He walks with an embarrassed shirk
and a shy smile, shepherding
his bunch of love-heart flowers
through the Valentine's Day mall.
He knows that flowers are a public paean
to women, public women's business
for the world abroad to see, and alien
therefore to men.

        And so he sidles
with his flowers, sidesteps
through the shopping crowd, knows
that what they're really thinking
is: 'What a good-sized bunch
of horticultural genitalia
he carries in his arms.
He's in with half a chance tonight –
a bunch the size of that
might drive a girl to frenzy!'

And he sidles on,
our man of flowers…
men and flowers always look
uncomfortable together.

The Marry-Go-Round

Obituary for June Allyson

She went for a dentist in the end,
a safe choice for her ageing years,
all passion well-concealed by then.
They always opt for firm ground
after the fun-fair, forgetting
with the late onset of missionary zeal,
the excitement of the roller-coaster,
the somersaults they turned in air.

Even marauding glamour-pusses
hunting offsets for their fading charms
seek suburban comforts in the end.
It's not just the wholesome Junes,
the nation's sweethearts. Her third time
on the merry-go-round, she sought
the quiet settled life; nothing Hollywood
about her final coupling, unspectacular
though highly planned. She regarded him
as her crowning achievement,
the dentist she went for in the end.

Painting the Edges

If it wasn't for the edges it'd be a snack,
painting the broad expanses, slapping it on.
But when you're pushed to the edge –
to tidy, to clarify, to put it straight
down the line – then you strike trouble.
There is need for care and time.
Here at the margins, the brushwork
must be fine, ritualised like dance,
the essence of life and work: defining
the space that shows our colours
in their brightest hue.

Orientallan

My open-hearted brother has gone
for two years overseas,
an ex-pat not a traveller,
taken his warmth and presence
away from home to wow them
in Hong Kong, to lay half of Asia
in his aisles. Let your heart
stay pointed home, reminding you
on bad days, Orientallan,
of the blue skies,
the olive gums,
the yellow beaches,
the racket of cicadas in summer.
And remember me, your brother
who shares your wandering soul,
in reverie on a morning train,
thinking of you
newly minted into Asia.

My Son from the South

For Murray

And now it approaches the time
when you will come home,
my son from the south.
Winter ages and grows old,
turns into spring, and you
move between cities
in your twenty-second year.
Your life turns too,
small calibrations on a grand scale,
slow-turning in these strong years
so that for a moment
you are one of the immortals,
a young god striding over landscape
one with the world, shaping it,
nothing ever beyond your grasp –
everything simply
a matter of will and time.

Cadet Day English Lesson

An assault on *Wuthering Heights*

At the four points of the classroom, they set up camp
to reconnoitre. This ground is unfamiliar,
this windy and wild riding of Yorkshire,
and the map of first impressions gapped and unreliable.

As the conscripts settle, the task of reconnaissance begins.
At first they ration intelligences gained from forays
through minefields of powerful prose, and test the wind:
will it be a pitched battle? Or ambush and subterfuge?

The councils of war are brief – the course charted,
munitions piled. A subtle campaign could last
all summer! Biting the issued bullets, the troops
marshal random thoughts and route march over Bronte.

Poem Pruning

For N R

Cut! Cut!

Prune and trim.
Snip the crown,
pare the brim!

Cut! Cut!

Nip and tuck.
Poetic surgery's
often luck.

Cut! Cut!

Never add.
One word good,
two words bad.

Film Fruit

For B B

Some stories, sweet as sugarplums
fall from the screen, but others
are the rancid fruit of nightmares.
Relieved now of ancient obligations
you can sit back with a chinking drink
and take your pick! The choice
of narratives is yours alone.
Half-grown plots abound
common as refrigerated apples
hackneyed as the woody pear.
Others show lack of proper nurturing,
should have been mulched carefully,
harvested for seeds or picked green,
turned and tended closely by hand
to ripen wonderfully. On some occasions
whole orchards can be planted with such stock.
Special stories, rare ones, lay down
the hungers of memory, are there for dreaming,
tantalising, conjuring the taste of paradise –
fragrant as pawpaw
quenching as watermelon
exotic and juicy as the magic
of the temptress mango.

Chas. Conder's Holiday

Bronte Beach, Queen's Birthday, 1888

People play in the middle distance.
Parents and child, centre-left,
celebrate the old Queen's birthday
in pink, blood-red and grey.
Why the unfurled umbrella –
the fierce white light or unseen rain?
Beyond them the Tasman heaves
dangerous and blue; the headland
shrugs its sandstone scarp.
This is the coast of New South Wales
in the centennial year,
an outskirt of empire.
Australia is only a concept –
ephemeral, shifting, monochrome –
waiting to be coloured in…
On this day in 1888
with a colonial English eye,
Conder brushstroked Bronte
in colours of Union Jack.

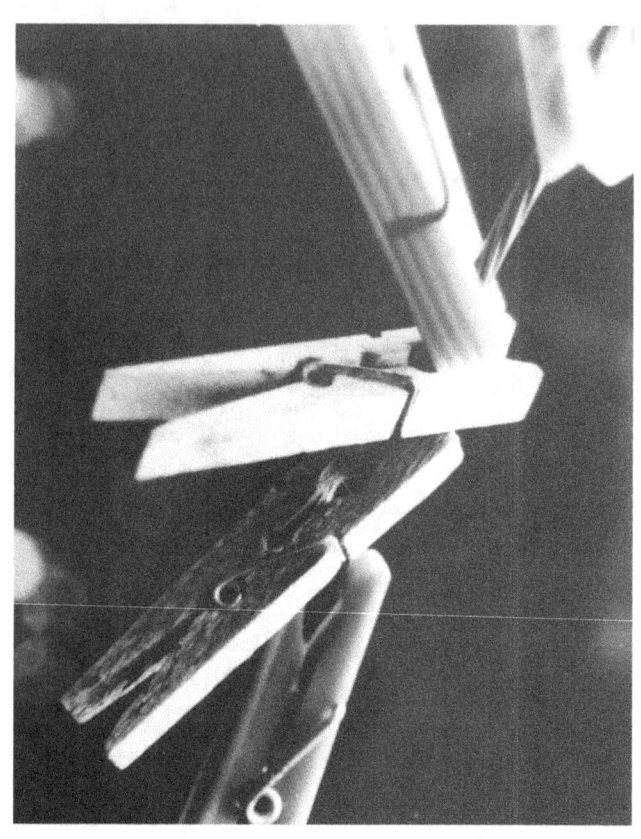

Peg Whorl

Their eyes
   the hollow core
      of wire springs

   this flock of gripping bird beaks
      clamping for the kill
         cartwheels overhead //

      now gymnasts on the high bar
         this tumbling troupe of acrobats
            begins from morning sun

         to spin a Fibonacci swirl
            a patterned curl of sunflower
               in arc of seeds / conjuring

         a crested plume of DNA
            a helix of honeycomb / the spiralling
               path of the bee //

These Artful Tarts

In all good galleries of art they lie in wait,
flirtatious wallgirls loose with their affections
bonding intimately with every marauding male.
Sexual or serene, ageless or edgy, out-there
or evergreen, dressed formally or dishabille,
sometimes entirely in the buff, they entrance,
enthral, imprison us…until in sweet remorse
we prise ourselves from their honeyed,
arty clutches and move on.
But shameless they are nonetheless,
faithless beauties, and we feel their betrayal
keenly, having bonded and given our hearts.
Even one furtive, over-the-shoulder glance
is enough to know they're at it again,
casting their amorous nets, seducing
all-comers with their cornucopias of charm.

Is There Any News?

The French king on his short last walk
with guards and gaolers at his side,
was worried less by his coming end
than the loss at sea of his grand design.
No clutch of courtiers round him then,
no word returned for several years –
the last dispatch from Botany Bay
before the troublesome coup occurred.
A last wish, Countrymen, if you choose…
Is there any news of La Perouse?

Policy Launch

From the front of the Four Seasons Room
across the faded green of winter carpet
a policy spring begins to bloom.
Coloured powerpoints too small to read
shine like sunlight on the room's front wall.
Speakers drone in monotone above
the nodding heads of invited guests
reciting frameworks and guiding principles.
How best to pollinate minds drifting
from the bright petalling of policy?

The man from the Institute begins with a joke
but falls soon into somnolent step, sowing
the policy context on winter ground.
From tiny holes, the policy itself spills seed.
In the background, glasses chink;
canapes and finger sandwiches
sprout from the kitchen on silver trays.
At the last, after formal blessings
from a Minister and senior bureaucrats,
new policy, like a shaky lamb,
goes forth into the world.

The Visit from the Queen

For John Dengate

He slaved away in the factory, my father,
working metal reluctantly for an absent Queen.
Tired of Menzies and the monarchist clap-trap,
he worked every day at his factory bench
in an act of unwelcome homage,
hands hard and skilled, scarred with acid
but his heart not in it as he cut and brazed
and hammered his way towards the Queen.

In Martin Place, his lanterns of bronze survive him,
suspended from the colonnade of the GPO.
I glance up always as I pass, looking at them
neat and aligned, all the work of his hands alone.
Proud of his trade, he knew his skill, my father…
and had a way with words as well.
I laugh now at what he thought of it all,
at the words he muttered in quiet protest
to me, to my mother, to his boss as well
and anyone else in earshot during
his eight months of royal toil:
'What if she doesn't look up?'

The Day that Gough Got In

'It's Time again…' beguiles Memory,
nailing us together on your back steps
at midnight, the day that Gough got in.

That Saturday in early summer
we were old enough to drive,
drink alcohol, die as conscripts
in the war, but barred by age
from polling booths abuzz.

We drove instead to a Sydney beach,
swam and splashed each other,
lay all afternoon on the hot sand,
salt baking in our hair. That evening
rubbing cream on our blistering skin,
we watched with your family
as the count came in, and cheered
as Gough announced his win.

That Saturday binds us still
wherever you are, always
the scent of skin cream,
the smell of salt in your hair.
We stand as then in the moonlit dark,
kissing goodbye to the old order
the day that Gough got in.

With a Small Pencil

It's how we change our government
or how we don't, with a small pencil
and two bits of paper, one clearly
more a bedsheet than a bit.
All over Girt-By-Sea, at cardboard booths we stand –
in school auditoriums, community centres,
council chambers and church halls.
There are mums and dads and grandads checking rolls,
initialling voting papers. And there's a young bloke
in casual clothes at the door ushering us forward.
Out front, we run the gauntlet of Party members
handing out 'Who-To-Vote-For' leaflets
which we take, or knock back, or gather
those we don't like for immediate disposal.
Out back, where the real party is, the local P and C
barbecues sausages, while stalls manned by parents
sell bric-a-brac, books that have seen many hands
and plants potted at home. There is order and laughter
in all of this, an informal sense of occasion,
an apparent lightheartedness that doesn't detract
from our serious intent. Over it all, the familiar
scent of freedom wafts like smoke from the barbecue.
The only uniforms in sight
are those of the local bushfire brigade
waiting in line to vote.

Small Things

Small things signal earthquakes –
a shift of air, a trail of ants,
the flinch of a lizard's eye.
His dying time was like that.

I knew again his beaky nose
sharpened by illness, his hair
brushed back, parted in the centre
like an out-of-fashion Lothario,
his lazy left eye sent walkabout
by the stroke. I could recognise
once more my own hands
in the familiar shape of his,
but after weeks in hospital,
his were soft and pale,
accentuating blood vessel
and scar.

Above all the small things
it was the voice, rooted in the bush
and the past, that made him real,
gave him the cadences of Curtin
and Chifley in the old newsreels,
Chips Rafferty on the screen:
'G'dye, mite… 'Ow are ya?' he said,
on the edge of his own history.

Two days beyond his death, the body
laid out in the funeral parlour,
it was his forehead cold against my lips
that told me the voice was gone,
vanished into the broad-vowelled past;
that, and the fact that his hair
for the first time ever in his life,
was parted strangely on the right.

Nothing Lasts

My father's notes in a 1959 cashbook
have long ceased to matter.
His face in an old photograph
flashing a gold tooth, fades
to the cold, grey face of the coffin.
(If ever he launched a whoop of joy,
I don't know what became of it).
That wooden school case he crafted
in the first summer of sixty-nine
is broken, swollen, decrepit now,
waiting in a garage corner
for the time of fallapart.

Nothing lasts. All things pass
and die, all feelings falter.
Time is a line, a piece of string,
not the clock's relentless circling.
Ticking dials deceive
by making time
seem tethered.

Picking Up the Sun

Out of the silences that are myself
through a dream that loops and curls,
my dead father swims beneath sun-glint
on lagoon water, holding his breath
for time beyond count.

I sense rather than see him
know he's there beneath
the water like a shark, close
but dangerous no longer.
Bursting then to air, his head
and shoulders break the surface
in a thousand splinters of light;
bright beads of water
fall in cascade from his hair.

His smile is unfenced, open.
Against blue sky and palm trees
he rises from the warm lagoon
alive again and young, his wars
now always over, gold tooth
forever picking up the sun.

Ontological Ouch!

He's reading a slim tome called *Enterprise Ontology*,
this bloke on the morning train beside me
deep in a chapter on 'The Organisation Theorem',
one mid-page flaunting, in separate coloured segments,
an isosceles pyramid annotated with corporation-speak.
It might keep him awake past Chatswood, that diagram –
but only if he places the open book between us on the seat,
imagines the pyramid standing upright from the page,
and plonks his backside down upon
its enterprising business end.

How to Make a Romantic Poet

To Charlotte Smith (1749–1806) and her scarce-remembered sisters:
'Indignantly is fled thy noble spirit.'

He must have a sister named Dorothy, a child called Harold
and a brother named Tom. He has to be either a virgin or a
rake, or somewhere in between, with a sublimated or possibly
uncontained Desire for his sister or half-sister. He needs to be
born in the late 18th century or early 19th into the prevailing
Zeitgeist of Revolution and Light. He must suffer from a
grab-bag of ailments and Idiosyncrasies such as consumption,
a club foot, a bankrupt estate, a compulsive Habit of sailing
in wild storms off Italian beaches, and be not averse to
burning drowned friends on the shore after rescuing their
hearts for burial elsewhere (see below). He should have an
over-fondness for Class A drugs -–or beakers full of the warm
South, at the very least. He must be willing to procreate
when he can with someone not legally entitled to bear his
children, then give them weird names and neglect them, or
pack them off to a boarding school in Switzerland. His
backyard must contain a lime-tree bower, he should wear an
albatross of some sort round his neck and have a nightingale
every evening sanctify his soul with its purity of song. It is
required sometimes that he starve to Death in a garret in
search of legendary status, or possibly choose to die fighting
for an inherited Culture on a foreign shore. Whatever the
option, and there are many, he must ensure it happens before
the age of 35 or thereabouts, and when it does, that he's
buried in Rome, ideally with his name not written on the
gravestone, or at worst, only written once in water. In terms
of Philosophy, he must consider Beauty to be always the

equal of Truth, or the other way round; that Time can be a moment to die on or an Eternity to endure. He should be half in love with easeful Death, sympathetic to the breaking of Nations, machines and Conventions, capable of decreeing stately pleasure domes, wandering o'er hill and vale like a solitary cloud, and able to hear the unheard melody of ghostly flutes across two Millennia. He must be particularly careful never to open the door to strangers when the act of creation is upon him.

In sum, our Romantic poet must worship Nature in place of God and through his work define an ecology of the Human Spirit abroad in the natural world. After that, when he has time, he can get back to appreciating the little things: frost at midnight, mist upon the moors and fruitfulness in all things, natural or human. Two final and most important qualifications: he must not be afraid of capitalising abstract nouns in a random Fashion wherever they occur; and unless he wants to be forgotten, He can never be a She.

Aegean Blue

I swam with you
most afternoons that summer
on a quilt of Aegean blue/
enjoyed you
byronically
saronically
cycladically/
quilted you far
from sporadically/
wrapped you in water
bright
with sunshine / body-
surfed
your coastline/
bedded you
in waves of brilliant blue.

Eternity – passing the baton

…time! There's plenty of

  ! There's plenty of time

    There's plenty of time!

      plenty of time! There's

        of time! There's plenty

          time! There's plenty of

            ! There's plenty of time

              There's plenty of time!

                plenty of time! There's

                  of time! There's…

Islands of the Circle

O

ringed
with islands
and blue sea, I stand amid
granite, dust, thornbush perched
on the one knobbly hill of this sacred island,
barren now. From the top of Delos, from the hub
of the Aegean, I see the Cyclades arrayed around me
like a wheel spinning on every horizon, with my
Delian self the axle pinning the islands to
this spot: these islands of circumference
islands of the rim, islands of the
circle, islands of the
almost perfect

O

Avocado Eve

Eve
& her Alpines
travel still in a train
compartment, alone with me
one December. Three stations
to the South she offers
a spoonful of avocado,
my first bite.

Coconut
tropic oil
the taste of earth
sliding on my tongue.
She draws the spoon back
and facing me in the early dark
lights another Alpine. Her smile
in the glow of that cigarette
promises an Eve in transit
avocado-ripe
with
possibilities.

The Emperor of Fish

Hail
to the Emperor
of Fish, who talks all day upon
his mobile phone, up to his gills and no good
while the tide of market ebbs and flows. His chatter
is all of prices, fluctuations, demand…and supply, the point
where he steps in – the middleman grown rich flicking parcels
of fish flesh, with little charm but money by the lobster pot, riches
by the creel. And home he goes each evening
to his palace on the hill,
whingeing
all the while
of government interference
and the fuckwits who write the rules.

We
watch him
across the room,
imagine him talking under water
waving his free hand about while strolling
amongst swaying tendrils of kelp, a rise of bubbles
streaming from his mouth…until at last, mid-sentence,
completely out of the blue, he's swallowed whole by the taxman
in the guise of a great white shark.

Cat Ritual

The bottomless cat pit
miaows for food
at the feet
of the great god Frigidaire.
In fervent circles
he prowls the kitchen
devout and
focused;

or

supplicant on furry haunches,
wails at the white high altar.

Snappy Tomasina, priestess
of the ritual, opens the god-fridge door
to genuflect, and take a metal offering
from the bottom shelf. Now,
in a frenzy of mewling and tabby fur,
she wields the ceremonial cutlery
and draws the cat noise after her
through the open
kitchen door.

Felinity

She cajoled in those
first flirtatious weeks,
curled round me
lissome and sinuous
rubbing my ear
stroking my ego.
She purred
and preened
and patted.

Later,
after the purring and patting
were done, and the spitting
and hissing to follow,
I'd learned how well
she scratched.

The Undeep Desk

Selected, point-in-time *graffiti* from university library desks, with a modicum of verbal glue

This is *the undeep desk i.e.*
no intellectual or theological arguments
here, just plenty of sex and scatology!
They tell me *sex is boring,*
that *mangoes are better than sex*
and while I wouldn't really know –
I'm a twenty year old virgin, you see –
I remain unconvinced, somewhat confused
by the range of my acquaintances, and uncertain
even of my gender and orientation.
I love Carol, but *I slept with Calvin Klein*
last night (a fashion statement – I remain intact).
I think I'm in lust with Rosa, however.
Rosa is a sex fiend. And then there's Lily.
Lily's as ugly as sin, but she'd still
give a dead man a hard-on! HELP me,
Carol, Calvin, Rosa, Lily! *I shall be free!*
This way to anonymity? Do I dare to eat a peach?
I suck trout's balls instead!

The Woman Who Had Her Head Detached

From a brief news report

I know what she may have felt,
this woman who had her head
detached by surgeons then realigned.
Work can cause the same affliction,
compel a permanent downward slant,
a long, slow skew –
with the process always piecemeal
before the weeks
close in like that.

Perhaps one day, a gifted surgeon
will come along and offer restitution –
deftly sever head from spine,
turn it gently a few degrees to the left
(where it used to be)
and arc it up sufficiently
to let me see the sky?

Crows in the City

Crows in the city caarck their carrion cries
over traffic at midday. What was that?
A crow? Shit! Stone the bastards!
They've invaded the metropolis
scavenging for food. Why are they here,
where they've never been before?
Drought? El Niño? Global warming?
Are they presagers of doom? Harbingers
of the hot dry times to come?

I have them at home now too,
in my little patch of suburban bush,
where they lord it over my back terrace
even when I'm there – game as accomplished
criminals, black as boot polish, devilishly clever.
They upend pot plants, uproot plant tags,
move seashells and white pebbles around,
dunk pieces of bread in bird-bath water
and leave me with a ratty assortment
of old chop bones picked clean,
shards of plastic and coloured glass,
useless trinkets picked up elsewhere.

In the city, I hear them from my office desk
over the conversation in progress,
over the traffic in the street below.
The corbies of Bridge Street
sqwaarck the afternoon away,
announce their Hitchcockian presence
in long staccato warnings
that echo through the streets.

The Courtesan and the Poet

They were both blonde when we bought them,
exquisitely carved – before such things were
mass produced. We saw them standing side by side
in Beijing, for sale as a couple – a courtesan and a poet –
and had them on display for twenty years, always
positioned on the sideboard together, turned slightly
toward each other, their glances crossing in front,
their black lacquered bases almost touching.

They aged together, the blonde wood burnishing
over time, until you stained them both some years ago
and they acquired a darker hue. Soon after,
we separated, dividing our possessions with little ado.
I assumed you'd take them both, and never
mentioned them amongst the chattels I desired.
But you took the courtesan alone, left me
the fat poet, divorced them with little thought.
Until that time they'd never been apart.

Freedom's Gate

Her least important tombstone
might seem her only legacy
her only peg in memory –
a plaque
in the shopping mall at Strahan
no grave
        no ashes
                no body

For decades now, every last
spark that Rozi was, every green
unbroken act of will,
have rolled her memory
in the rushing deep of Denison
that same age of nineteen
every year
        every day
                every moment
since the raft spun and tipped
and the river sucked her down
beneath its whirling skin

Her main tombstone
speaks nothing of death at all,
wild and untamed as it was
when it made her part of it,
dissolved her suddenly
in its heart.
At one with the wilderness,
her absence
has no meaning here.
Her presence,
constant,
makes it real.

That Summer of the Bicentenary

At the start of that summer on the sloping hillside
we walked beneath wheeling seagulls and amongst
gravestones luminous as marble lanterns;
beyond, in the distance, the summer blue of sea
infiltrated the long calm. For two hours
late on that vivid afternoon it was death
that we denied and the chill air of parting,
walking our last steps together
in a marble twilight of blackened crypts
and angels with broken wings.

Luminous the headstones were and bright
the desperate surge of your love, flaming
into the last hours as night came on, surreal
and sentient, flaring as we wandered
hand in hand, and together hip to hip,
through the paths of the other dead.

Bitter Days

Only cold stone
bitten blue by winter wind,
a bank of fern:
a memory of you
grown spare as sky
through the poplar's winter frame.

Even so,
most nights are kind
and dark is loath to feed
too long upon your memory.
It is only cold stone
that brings it back,
lump-like and late
on bitter days.

Perhaps You Went Quietly

For R S

Perhaps you went quietly into oblivion
with no smell of gas, exhausted by love
that broke your grip and you fell to this pass
one evening in your car, a length
of rubber tubing carefully deployed ?
Or possibly, at the last, there was nothing
quiet about it. You foamed and raved,
crushing the brittle pieces of your life
to dust like Christmas baubles?
Whichever it was, it hardly matters now.
Nothing can touch you – not hand or eye,
not thought or feeling. All are helpless
to penetrate the barrier you embraced
that evening, watching the distant lights
tremble in the blackness. You must
have chosen such a vista for your death,
such a great divide from earth,
such a distance to witness as you went,
as consciousness withered and flickered
in the surrounding dark, as each
trembling light went slowly out.

Last Vacation

In old age they come deluging in, the memories –
uninvited avalanche, welcome but prohibiting sleep.
The mind is getting its house in order, taking stock,
reviewing, introducing those acquaintances
kept distant by time, place or preference,
thawing the frozen images of each person,
flooding the previously impenetrable barriers.
People who never knew each other converse and play.

There are no borders between memories now,
no restrictions on travel, no visas or passports.
Memory itself is having its last vacation,
knowing that death has booked its window seat
and travels along for the ride.

Love in the Time of Coronavirus

In the checkout queue, almost idly
I think of you, in the caterpillar crawl
of shopping trolleys, in this regulated pause
between the gathering and the reckoning.
I reach back wondering, imagine you
in a similar queue – masked – musing
on the order and rhythm of your life
as you enact its altered rituals.

And suddenly, in this fraught
but mundane harvesting of groceries, I hunger
for disorder again, for the newness of you,
for the temptations of undiscoveredness,
for that first fizz of just-opened love
that buoyed us on its updraft
before it all went viral.

You on Patmos

How do I know what Patmos is like,
apart from traveland splotches of blue
and white, and the odd erratic donkey?
The landscape is all of my making
as I put you into it from the overnight ferry.

You on Patmos, blue Aegean you,
in my mind's eye standing now
a tourist on a pilgrim shore, no hint
of apocalypse clouding your days.
Through the same lens I see
all things I imagine Patmos has:
white heat of bright summer,
water blue as the thought of melting ice,
rocky footpaths through gnarled olives,
the noise of donkeys braying dust
at hillsides of ancient rock,
men in the market square playing cards,
tobacco smoke wreathing weathered ouzo faces,
children singing, women in black,
windmill sails white against an ageless ocean.
All this I fear possessing you,
compelling you to stay like other Mediterranean
wanderers who've walked before you there,
trapped in a timeless lethargy of paradise.

But, as I place myself beside you
a stranger on that shore
      waiting for your tide to turn,
I look ahead and fortunately
      see you leaving Patmos
          soon.

Town of Boeotia

From Delphi it is merely a town on the road to Athens,
a place on the map where people have lived since the Bronze Age,
always with a bustling, narrow main street, rich farms
and fertile olive-growing land. In ancient times
it was part of the territory of Boeotia.

Generations have grown up and lived here
like anywhere else, and down the long arcade of years
people have died in its vicinity, victim to all kinds of weapons,
accidents, the odd pandemic and the normal process of life.
Since the last war, its fertility rate has been well above
the national average and its climate hospitable
the whole year round, although two months every winter
become a little cold.

In spite of all this, and to the local mayor's chagrin,
the town has no monuments worth speaking of
and no archaeological sites worth visiting,
not even the ruins of a medieval castle for road signs
to pick out and tourist guides inflate…
nothing important ever happened here.

Postcard From Tuscany

It is wet and 4 degrees outside
driving to Assisi and Arezzo –
a landscape misty and brown,
shading to olive green.
In the distance, dotted
with one little town after another,
a wash of low hills.
Many leafless trees line my roads.

I paint you with me
into these winter colours
but you refuse to fit,
locked in your Sydney summer.
I hope you are well,
my family – and between
beach and harbour
and evening barbecues,
remember who I am.

Barbarians Inside the Gates

Unexpectedly at night the skirl of bagpipes
scuds across the stones in Piazza del Popolo…
the twin churches hide their darkened frowns.
The chanter's out of tune, the execution's wanting
and the passing crowd begins to shy away.
The obelisk Augustus brought from Egypt
contorts into hieroglyphic scowl, muttering
a pharaoh's curse: May your mother
grow testicles before your birth!

Standing Stones

They are human…'converted into stane by ane Inchanter' and set up in a ring…'for devotione'. – John Morisone, Isle of Lewis, around 1680.

From flesh and blood, the Inchanter
has translated them to stone, planted them
in tight circles for ancient devotions.
These weathered rings of giants cling
stubbornly to scrubby knolls at the side
of ocean lochs, lashed by the onslaught
of Atlantic gales. They become huge flutes,
low-pitched drones, rocky sentinels
catching the cold blast across water,
across the treeless Hebridean hills,
howling on the world's western fringe.
On gentler days from depths unknown,
they keen low orisons for vanished souls,
for the worlds they knew now gone.

But yet they persist.
They have another life.
Each summer, the Inchanter brings them back,
wakes them from the old sleep and spirits them,
human again, to city parks and sports grounds,
to competition fields, dresses them in tartan
with bagpipes shouldered and drums suspended.
They pay for their parole,

earn their keep, at attention stand
and compete for glory against others
of their kind on the days
they bear the spell
more lightly.

Inside concentric rings
these avatars of enchanted stone
voice the ancient music of their kind,
fingers fluttering in summer gusts, mouths
and cheeks blowing and bulging, forcing the wind
back upon itself before the spell of stonelock
falls once more upon them.

With their brief summer gone,
they find themselves replanted on the treeless hills,
another winter to be endured on the world's
wild fringe. The promise of summer glory
is hidden now, dormant, buried deep
in igneous DNA – but the flint will strike
and the stone will wake again,
whenever the Inchanter
divines the perfect moment
to warm and rouse the blood.

Killin

For Anne, David, Kim and James Gray

Here the centuries run like seconds, skies of cloud
and countless suns scud in time-lapse overhead.
Long swathes of time etch their histories
on the hillsides, the stones of the river bed…
This valley gouged by ice felt one day
the thaw begin, grew gradually green, inhabited –
and echoes now this summer
with the bleating of black-faced sheep.
When did the last ice melt away and the glacier
leave its footprint here, this small deep loch
holding in silence its complement of brown trout
and the elusive char? Such questions disappear
in the wind at night through Henry's wood,
or dissolve in the brown water rounding old stones,
the river's slow revenge on glacial imprisonment.
Here the summer dark is brief and light,
laughter and stories dance together in the Lodge…
but in winter, if the mood is right,
the ice will reassert itself and whip
the length of glen to gale, from the blind
face of Strone to Garrogie's spruce towers.
Each winter brings this inkling back of what
once was, a cold hackling in the early dark
of how things were in time before remembering.

Poolside at the Bali Grand

Lying poolside at the Bali Grand
half-shaded on my banana lounge,
I feel the tropical sun frying both feet.
The top half is blocked with 15 plus
but not my legs, which were in shade –
until in sleep the sun swung round.

Here by banks of blazing bougainvillea
and rampant sprays of palm fronds,
children frolic on the waterslide.
A butterfly skitters
over pale red hibiscus flowers.
The sounds of water splashing,
children running, bathers plunging
fill the polyglot morning
in this holiday community of transients.

Down the chute, watersliding children
scream and yell to recumbent parents,
can never understand the adult need
for quiet vegetation. Too loudly they scream
like the bougainvillea.

                        No!
I don't want to slide
and scream and shout,
splashing into the green water
with potent eruptions of noise.
I want to touch the water gently,
caress it – and slip quietly unseen
beneath the surface of this
lavish, tropical holiday.

The Next Island

Here by this blue island pool,
Bali: domesticated waterfalls
and clatter of the world
at play. Beneath it all
untamed, the quiet roar
of ocean on reef.

Under nodding triangles
blue prahus skim
beyond wavebreak.
The sun's heat warms
my already sunburnt leg.
This island has meant
ten days of time-drift,
respite from oceans of work
with more to chart and sail.

To the east,
across the deepest strait in the world,
lies Lombok, the next island.

Beijing Ascending

For Rosemary and Laura

We spent all day getting to the top of things –
climbing stairs, hauling on balustrades
lifting our aching legs
up one incline and then another:
the pagoda
the drum tower
the bell tower
the emperor's favourite resting place
on top of the wooded mountain…
So that, by the end of the day
with dusk descending, exhausted
we realised too late that though we'd climbed
the tourist climbs and come down again
in one mad skelter, we'd failed completely
to get to the bottom of anything at all.

Tai Hu

Wuxi, China

Although the trees are leafless now
and a cold wind blows off the lake,
men in ragged overcoats
cast nets for winter fish.

As we cross the bridge of stone
circling in air, I look back
into the sun's face and see
two children, black shapes waving,
small against the vastness of Tai Hu.

Tai Hu is shimmering silk
behind them, gold in the late afternoon
drawing thread from the sun's cocoon.
Almost spent, its warmth fails
to muzzle the wind's teeth.

The Open Window

At traffic lights
through the open window,
hands reach in
tapping my shoulder.
Other hands hold
ragged children
or stretch out
towards me
palms upward
imploring,
voices at my ear.
I can roll
the window up
against the hands
against the voices
but not
against the eyes.

Other Voices

1. Ritual

at the sink I stand
twice daily
propping on both arms
watching my life
in the wash
foam and swirl
watching my life
ebb and flow
my life in water
drain away

                this routine
                this loss in water
                this slow
                disappearing act
                has taken weight
                of ceremony

                                from dull routine
                                from trickling death
                                I've fashioned
                                Ritual

2. Thirteen Summers

What right had you to leave
the years you failed to live
untenanted? To leave me
floundering in the shallow
pool of belonging, while the days
and years skim past
churning the waves to froth?
I know that you
had scarcely learned to swim –
that thirteen summers is hardly
time to feel the water –
but how am I expected
to strike out for the other side
alone?

3. The Twenty-second of July

This is now my home,
this space, this light,
this land – but never
as though there were
no other.

My children have sprung
from it – it lives in them
as they move and breathe.
And now I am of it too
but always from another,
schooled at first through years
with the map
still etched in red.

With the present stronger,
more complex,
each year at this time
the past strengthens too:
these years are all
trunk, branch and leaf
but those remain
my solid roots.

4. The Stone Unburdens

I am only what I am,
and with time, less even than this:
sea-gritted, pitted-with-salt
fragment of Sicily, of her heart –
cold tear of Etna plucked
from the suck and wash of waves.

Now this humble lump of stone,
once my heart would sear your hand
and my light unshadowed burn
your retinas to the brain. With the elements
I was eternal in the birth-bright moment,
everything and nothing,
passionate, unyielding.

But moments pass and yielding comes.
I am what yielding brings, and the limits
I live within lie hard in your hand
as sea and time have fashioned them,
solid, cold and dull. Even so,
there are shadows that have tongues
and silences that speak if you
will let them tell – of lustres lost,
of passions choking crusty veins,
and of the ache in darkness
for the fire that is dead.

Remember me for what I was
and know that all things hard
are not inscrutable – that hard things
all knew fire once, and though burnt out,
are haunted by the radiance of their birth.

5. The Spirit in the Clay

Sometimes, easily fired, I wheel
and turn on those who've thrown me,
only to crack and break
in pieces on the floor.
There, shattered and sharp,
even the smallest slivers
shrive, and sound as one
for shroud of clay.

6. If All Goes Well

When I was first put here, that tree was green –
three weeks ago when they stitched me inside,
brought me out to this veranda
and told me to stay in bed for five months.
Now the leaves are yellowing and the first to go
have gone, fluttering and spinning their way
to the gravel drive. Other women on this veranda
have also gone, thrust finally into motherhood
and allowed to take up their lives again, the stagnant weeks
behind them. I am still here and must watch
all those leaves turn and fall, and then stare
at the bare boughs and winter sky interminably, and wait
until the buds appear and thicken and at last unfold.
Then I too will bring forth new life, if all goes well.

7. Books Closing Down Sale

Across Pitt Street, balloons and streamers
inflict their colours on the world.
El Cheapo Books flogs dog-eared remainders
in a last ditch stand, closing down
this week in May. Alone and sullen,
I sit and stare as dusk-brink shoppers idle in
and lit shop fronts begin to hold the night.
This death is hard to bear, this wind at night
cold in my face. Our affair at its arse-end
has whimpered out, and I am wrung out,
hung unspread to harden, a tightly twisted
lump of nothing much at all.
I try to pretend that I'm all right and go
home to my wife and kids and smile.
Passing couples chatter, grow and fade.
Figures rifle through the piles of bargain books.
But all I know and feel is you as the darkness
settles in with this year's first chill wind.
I am inert. I cannot move.
How the fuck can I pretend composure?

On the Chemo

I wait for these days on the chemo to end,
for the half-drugged nights, above all, to be over,
sitting late for the needle and the nausea tablets,
burning inside, unable to lie and sleep.

I am not myself. Something with a mystery
at its heart eats away at me, and the chemo
eats away at it. I am a war zone,
a battleground, an uncivil landscape

of crooked cells, of bald head and scarred body
preparing to take up my life where it left off
or strike out on astonishing new roads –
again to become a person, but never the one I was.

Life will not be softly and sedately taken up again
as it was before the cancer and the chemo.
The old life is dead now, killed off; and the new life
unknown yet, but waiting furious engagement.

Borrowed Time

One night after illness, I dreamt of time in store
as though it were a commodity, a finite nugget
of precious metal, raw and misshapen,
held in the hand of some god I didn't believe in
and about to be snatched away in one sudden
descent into darkness. But then, miraculously,
just before waking, I discovered my time to come
newly minted, stamped out fresh and clean
in front of me, each day formed and whole,
all the days to come lined up before me
at the other end of sleep, like a highway
of new gold coins stretching on and on
in front of me, and out of sight.*

* I acknowledge a similarity in the ending to a line of Siegfried Sassoon's poem 'Everyone Sang': '…Winging wildly across the white/ Orchards and dark-green fields; on-on-and out of sight'.

The Idea of God

Yes.   Still an atheist,
I've not found God.   No.
I've not been looking for him either,
and God has not found me.   You ask
as though God lurks in illness, lies in wait
as the body goes awry.   It's people
who spin his presence out of air when most in need,
fashioning something inside themselves
where nothing was, some selvedge
of hope on the edge of despair.

Yes.   Some do achieve
communion with their own Almighties,
their individual architectures of God, believing
the voices resounding inside their Father's mansions,
the patriarchal palaces in which their Gods reside.
But it's the emptiness they feel
that speaks to them, the lonely spaces
they fill with their own imaginings.

No.   My loneliness
and the fears I walk within are a kind of solitude,
a godless freedom that only being finite brings,
striving for life moment by moment. The tongues
that speak to me are fellow spirits close by, or across
the distances of time, geography and circumstance,
who cannot imagine
voices other than human ones
to soothe and walk beside them
to the grave.

The Universe Within

For Chris

If what matters is not out there beyond us but within –
whether or not we think the soul outlasts our mortal
beings - I'm sure our spirits drink and sustain
themselves at a common source when they
roam and gather, no doubt tapping into
the great music of the universe
before coming back to share
what wisdom they
have learned.

If any great secrets do exist, I know the ones
that matter are not like that at all, not
things out there brought back but
the sudden joys that spring
unbidden from within,
when the voices
of creation
begin to
sing.

Still Clasped About the Stone

Here, rough-hewn, is precision
that eludes the eye,
and something more.
It is what it looks,
a messy core of flint
ridged and edged untidily.
If there is pattern, it usurps the stone.

But let the hand embrace it,
turn it slowly, feel it blend
and meld, it becomes an extension
of the hand with fingers falling
comfortably in hollows, and ridges
fitting neatly the folds of flesh.

As I hold it, its shape
a perfect fit in my large hand,
I am aware of my intrusion,
my trespass – the presence
of its maker and users
palpable as its weight and form.
I feel the grip of vanished fingers,
an absent hand in the space of mine
still clasped about the stone.

Termite

Like a termite
time gnaws away
starts to eat us
quickly   gathers pace
          chews
and spits us at the universe

It nibbles north   time
against gravity
through feet   legs   genitals
          stomach
heart   larynx   eyes   head
all they mean   falling away
sloughing off   until
at end there is nothing
no thing –
not   hinge
or screw

Feet go first
and walking   kicking fate
swimming against tide
and streamflow

Then legs
our essence now
upon the earth like lizards
no towers
to push us heavening

Genitals then   wet
hard against hope   with them
succour, slew of smiles   blast
of warm stars   exploding no more
in joy or betrayal

Stomach then   solidity and strength
ample meals   laden tables
hunger now full at bay
beyond   the world fold

Next the heart   uncharted
on open ground   falls prey
feels itself consumed   but can
no longer bleed   nor yearn   nor break

Larynx then   and the need
to sing and shout
rage against the dying…but cords
fray   dumbstruck

Eyes and ears next   the sound
of darkness falling   the long night
we all curl up in   drawing down
                cloaking
souls   alone

And in the end
nothing
but the spark   of thought
before the moment
when light   dies   becomes
again darkness   like
the start
Termite time turns south
           then
begins again
to remake
another world   another
fear of death

Dark Harbour

This ship sliding on the dark
reveals itself in silhouette
through glass – distant, silent
one light winking exhortation
to the chill September sky.

It slips from sight too soon
this ship, this vessel, this presence
on the dark unfathomable harbour,
on the black water of time,
one light blinking and flashing…
our brief cargo of days
beating against the growing dark.

Last Light

A still point at dusk,
a level surface of water,
a green mirror laid flat.

Immersed, I swim without
disturbing the still sheen
of polished water.

At peace, I become
one with the water,
vanish into the last light
that gilds its skin.

The Art of Hoping

IM David Hope

Our friendship began
with poetry, a decade ago,
a class at the WEA

in Bathurst Street –
you grey-bearded, artist-capped
seeking mysteries

of the patterned
word, and vagabond souls
attuned like yours.

You found me there,
another as well – and three of us
gathered then from time

to time, in coffee shops
with sheaves of half-formed poems,
uttering incantations

to each other
over tea, and the milkshake
you preferred.

Then one day
you vanished into silence
until Katrina's call

after your stroke –
about the time my postcard
from the Taj Mahal

caught up with you,
pinned to the nursing home
wall, where you lay

imprisoned by
circumstance, railing silently
against loss of speech

and movement, fiercely
determined to walk again, to get
the old life back

regain your work,
the freedom of two spindly legs
and the little money

your art brought in.
In nursing home, in hostel care,
later in your own

public housing, the struggle
against gravity consumed you,
and the need to keep

what order you could
amongst your few possessions.
And slowly you began

to win, with nothing
except your power of will, and
hunger deprived of art.

You talked, and read,
you walked with frame
and through it all

cried out your need
for ideas, books and conversation,
your interest

in almost everything
that danced through the rich
collage of your life…

model-maker, poet,
sculptor of miniatures, multi-
media bower-bird.

Now, between
the moments we remember you,
time ticks on,

struggling to fill
the space you've left amongst us…
And here we are

partners and family,
children of your flesh and spirit,
your clutch of friends

all of whom
in their several ways
looked out for you.

O vagabond fellow,
old spirit, my friend –
in what grand collage

of present and past
are you hiding now? Where
has time secreted you?

Acknowledgements

Some of these poems have previously appeared in newspapers, journals, anthologies and on websites, including *Westerly* (UWA), the annual *fourW* anthologies (CSU Wagga Wagga, NSW), publications of the former Poets Union, NSW (*Sun and Sleet, Prismatics, Untilted, Ask the Rain, Dodecahedron*), *The Mozzie* (Qld), *Pain and Renewal*, Vita Brevis Press, (USA); Silver Birch Press (USA); Black Bough Poetry (Wales); and *The Scottish Banner* (Australia, Scotland, USA).

Five chapbooks published over 2021–22 by Ginninderra Press – *Picking Up the Sun* (Picaro Poets), and *Frivolous*, *Australian Minuscule*, *Rattling Cutlery* and *Affinities* (Pocket Poets) – have also included some of these poems.

'The Courtesan and the Poet' won the 2022 poetry competition at McMahons Point in Sydney, held in association with the Sculpture at Sawmillers prize and exhibition, and related thematically.

My thanks go to the many friends who have shown interest and provided encouragement over the years – and suffered quietly while some of these poems were inflicted on them. I want to acknowledge specifically Bronwyn Boekenstein, Chris Bradshaw, Brian Davies, Rosemary Milkins, Philip Porter, Wayne and Val Sawyer and Sally Stewart for their assistance in putting together this selection of poems. In addition, colleagues from the North Shore Poetry Project, led by Philip, commented on a number of earlier drafts of particular poems.

An important thank you also to Stephen Matthews and Brenda Eldridge of Ginninderra Press for the opportunity of publication, their encouragement in doing so, and the considerable efforts they make in bringing Ginninderra Press poetry publications to fruition.

www.ingramcontent.com/pod-product-compliance
Lightning Source LLC
Chambersburg PA
CBHW071009080526
44587CB00015B/2396